★ *A Kid's Guide to the Economy*

Manfred G. Riedel

A Kid's Guide
to the
Economy

★ *illustrated by Ric Estrada*

Prentice-Hall, Inc. ★ Englewood Cliffs ★ N.J.

For the children I love: Nicholas Adler,
Karen and Laura Darby, Alice and Robert
Kunito, Bettina and Matthias Querfeld,
Cordula Riedel, and Rachel Stires.

Prentice-Hall International, Inc., London
Prentice-Hall of Australia, Pty. Ltd., North Sydney
Prentice-Hall of Canada, Ltd., Toronto
Prentice-Hall of India Private Ltd., New Delhi
Prentice-Hall of Japan, Inc., Tokyo

10 9 8 7 6 5 4 3 2 1

Library of Congress Cataloging in Publication Data

Riedel, Manfred G   1937–
   A kid's guide to the economy.
   Includes index.
   SUMMARY: A guide to basic economic ideas
explaining such terms as recession, taxes, and mo-
nopoly, and showing how they relate to everyday
life.
   1. Economics—Juvenile literature. [Economics]
I. Estrada, Ric. II. Title.
HB171.7.R464   330   75-35663
ISBN 0-13-515130-9

★ Table of Contents

★ *A Kid's Guide to the Economy*

Manfred G. Riedel

1 ★ Introduction

Although the ancient Greeks invented the word, "economy" couldn't be more up-to-date. It means how to make and spend wealth.

(To be a stickler, it means how to produce, distribute, and consume goods and services.)

Amazingly, economy affects almost every part of your life: Whether you get orange juice or a vacation, and what your home is like, depends on the economic health of your family and your country.

Because economy deals with how people share riches, it forces you to think:

Is it fair that some people or countries are wealthy and others are poor?

Should everyone have *total* freedom to get rich?

Is wealth only money—or is happiness wealth too?

Are we overworking the earth?

These are only a *few* of the important questions economy raises!

2 ★ *What Makes You Rich?*

Hamilton, Penny, and Tony were raking leaves to earn money. "How do you get rich?" asked Hamilton, mopping his brow.

"You need NATURAL resources, like land," answered Penny, leaning on her rake. "Land has everything. It produces crops. You can raise cattle on it. You might even strike oil."

"I don't even own a desert," Hamilton whispered sadly.

"Penny's goofy," said Tony. "What good is growing tomatoes if you can't make them into spaghetti sauce? What good are cattle unless you have meat-packing plants to turn them into hamburgers? What good is crude oil without refineries to make gasoline? People or countries need CAPITAL to be rich. Capital means the money and materials you put into factories and equipment. Capital makes natural resources useful and produces more wealth."

Spaghetti sauce! Put all capital into dogfood factories!

3 ★ *What Makes You Richer?*

"I don't have any capital," sighed Hamilton, "no cash, no factories, not even a shovel."

"PEOPLE are resources too," said Penny. "You can sell your muscles or brains."

"My muscles and brains!" shrieked Hamilton.

"Not *real* muscles or brains, silly," laughed Penny, "skills, if you're a carpenter, or knowledge, if you're a scientist. That's what we are doing now—selling our raking power!"

"Keep raking!" shouted Tony and Hamilton together.

Hey! What about dog power!

4 ★ *From Riches to Rags*

"Maybe Penny *is* goofy," said Hamilton. "Can't you run out of natural resources?"

"Sure—they can become SCARCE," answered Tony. "Penny could regrow crops or raise new cattle, even though it would take time. But if she ran out of oil, that would be *it!* Capital is safer."

"You can lose capital too," argued Penny. "What if you invested your capital in something stupid—like Conestoga wagons or whalebone corsets that nobody wants anymore?"

"I guess people are the only safe resource," decided Hamilton.

"You can't even bet on people," sighed Tony. "Look at how many nitwits kill themselves off in auto accidents. Others drop out or are too old or sick to work."

"Gee, can't you count on *any*thing in this life?" groaned Hamilton.

Waste not, want not.

5 ★ Who Gets to Chop Down the Trees?

"Too bad most of our *natural* resources are PRIVATE PROPERTY," said Penny. "A selfish person could chop down all the trees, ruin the landscape with strip mining, or pollute rivers. Resources should be PUBLIC PROPERTY, protected by the government."

"That's socialism!" Hamilton shrieked. "We capitalists believe in private property."

"Besides," Tony said, "socialist governments also chop down trees, strip mine, and pollute."

"If the *capital* resources were public," Penny persisted, "the government would invest wisely, not in silly whalebone corsets."

"What if a dumb government produced only underwear and no TV sets?" yelled Tony.

"And *people!*" shouted Hamilton. "I don't want to be public property. I want to do my own thing."

"Man! I never thought of that!" admitted Penny. "How could I be a balloonist if the government ordered me to be a Florence Nightingale?"

Everything should be public—except, of course, my territory.

14

6 ★ Why Susan and Andy Became Capitalists

Susan wanted to make money with her private capital of seven dollars. With this money she would found the Great Owl Company to produce owl paperweights.

"You can work for me," Susan told Andy. "Find twenty smooth, round stones and paint owl faces on them. I'll give you brushes and paint and pay you thirty cents for every paperweight you make. Don't worry about selling them; that's my risk. And if you get bored or tired, you can quit any time."

"Susan's not doing this out of love. She needs my skills for her own PROFIT," Andy thought when he accepted the offer. "But she's not twisting my arm—it's my own decision. It's everyone for himself under CAPITALISM. What have I got to lose?"

You might get fired.

7 ★ Why Peter and Alice Preferred Socialism

"Who wants to be a selfish capitalist like Susan?" said Peter. "Paperweights are a nice decoration, but let's produce something society really needs—like potholders."

"Yes, we should think of other people's needs, not just of our own profit," agreed Alice. "And instead of one person being the boss, we'll set up a cooperative and SHARE everything—the cost of supplies, the labor, and the income from our sales. That's SOCIALISM."

Since they were sharing everything, Peter and Alice agreed that it would be unfair to the other if one person didn't do his or her share. So they made a pact—no backing out.

Do you get to share the misery too?

8 ★ *Who Got Ripped Off?*

After Andy spent an hour finding twenty smooth, white stones and three hours painting owls on them, Susan gave him six dollars. "Not bad," Andy thought. "That comes to a dollar fifty an hour."

But then Susan sold all the paperweights for seventy-five cents apiece in only one hour. The brushes and paint had cost her only one dollar.

"You earned eight dollars and didn't even work hard!" Andy screamed. "You've exploited me!"

Meanwhile, Alice knitted sixty potholders while Peter fooled around and made only twenty. But when they sold all eighty potholders for fifty cents each, Peter happily pocketed his full half of the forty dollars.

"That's not sharing everything equally," yelled Alice. "I've been exploited."

Man is only 500,000 years old—Maybe he'll find a perfect system in the next 500,000 years!

19

9 ★ A Big Joke

"Socialism just doesn't work," said Susan, counting her money. "Too many lazy people won't do their share."

"Capitalism isn't so super, either," retorted Peter. "Too many greedy people grab too much."

"But isn't it absurd that socialist countries had to encourage production by adding some *capitalism?*" laughed Susan. "To reward the harder workers, the Soviet government lets farmers who finish their public work raise cattle and corn to sell for their own profit."

"So what?" said Peter. "Capitalist nations had to add some *socialism!* Because the poor were starving, the United States started public welfare programs, like giving out food stamps. Because the rich were hogging the best beaches and mountains, the government had to create public lands like Yellowstone National Park."

"What a joke!" agreed Susan and Peter.

Not as funny as a shaggy-dog story!

21

10 ★ Hamilton Can't Make Money Without a Supply

On his Florida vacation, Hamilton became addicted to a Florida specialty, wild orange pie. So he brought home a big sack of wild oranges. Then he began to make wild orange pies and sell them.

"Everyone is nuts about your pies, Hamilton," Penny said. "You'll be a millionaire!"

"Dream on!" Hamilton sighed. "I've just used up all my wild oranges. If I don't find a new SUPPLY, it won't matter how much people like my pies. I just won't have anything to sell."

Penny and Hamilton dashed to all the supermarkets but couldn't find wild oranges. Hamilton's business was over.

Make flea pies. You'll never run out of fleas!

11 ★ Andy Can't Make Money Without a Demand

When Andy's dog had eleven puppies, Susan cried excitedly, "You can make a lot of money by selling these puppies. Everyone in the neighborhood loves dogs."

Andy hammered a big sign: "Puppies for sale, $2 each." In no time he sold seven puppies. Then DEMAND dwindled. Andy lowered his price. But nobody else wanted a puppy.

"I forgot that some people already have dogs," said Susan when Andy complained.

Andy had a hard time *giving away* the rest of the puppies for nothing!

Sell dogfood. It's irresistible!

12 ★ Penny Goes From Good to Best

"How can I compete with Hamilton?" Penny sobbed after the block party. Penny had hoped to sell her homemade wooden bookends for two fifty a pair. But next to her, Hamilton also sold bookends—and he charged only a dollar fifty a pair. No wonder people didn't flock to Penny's stand! "COMPETITION is terrible!" wailed Penny.

Thinking hard, Penny came up with an idea. She would paint her bookends in bright colors. At the next block party, Penny was a big success. "Look at Penny's beautiful bookends," people kept saying. And this time they bought all of her bookends for two fifty. "Competition is great," beamed Penny. "It caused me a lot of work, though."

"Wise up!" Tony advised. "Instead of knocking yourself out, get *rid* of the competition. Get a MONOPOLY— total control over your market. Then you can charge whatever you want and not worry that someone's going to offer a better product."

It's a dog-eat-dog world.

13 ★ *The Savvy Few*

"Monopolies are evil," objected Penny. "Without competition you can gyp customers, exploit workers, and even bribe politicians."

"Without competition you might earn more," Tony said stubbornly. "What if you put your extra profit into research, better pay for workers, or donated a museum to the community?"

"Yok-yok, who's that noble?" laughed Penny. "That's why antitrust laws outlawed monopolies. I wouldn't want to do anything illegal."

"Then try an OLIGOPOLY," suggested Tony. "That's not illegal."

"A whaaaaatt?" asked Penny.

"When only a *few* producers—only you and Hamilton, for example—control the market, you have an oligopoly," Tony explained. "If you both make similar bookends and charge about the same price, you can divide the market peacefully instead of hassling each other. It's not as powerful as a monopoly—but not as tough as cutthroat competition, either!"

"Sounds wicked to me," said Penny, "even if it *is* legal."

You scratch my back, and I'll scratch yours.

26

14 ★ *Uncle Sam to the Rescue!*

"Pioneers didn't have laws against capitalism," complained Tony. "Daniel Boone could do as he pleased."

"How many people farm or hunt as Daniel Boone did?" asked Penny. "Things have changed, and today most of us *buy* food. Capitalism had to change too, to protect consumers. What if some monopoly took over the wheat market and raised prices so high that hardly anyone could afford bread? To protect us, the government *had* to make antitrust laws."

"And Abraham Lincoln's mother died," said Hamilton, "from drinking bad milk. Now the Food and Drug Administration and other consumer agencies protect us against bad food and products."

"Pioneers were litterbugs too," said Penny. "When they messed up a place, they just moved West. With the frontier gone where can we escape if others mess up the environment? So we have pollution controls."

"Aaargh!" groaned Tony. "For total freedom you need a new frontier!"

Try Mars!

15 ★ Andy Discovers That Money Costs Money

"When you borrow money it's called CREDIT," said Susan as she counted out ten five-dollar bills. "Dad gave us a fifty dollar credit."

"Yippee!" yelled Andy. "Now we can buy the oil lamps at the flea market, fix them up, and make a fortune the next time the electric power fails. We'll pay your dad back his fifty dollars in no time."

"You think credit is free?" asked Susan. "We have to pay Dad interest—that's like rent on the money. Dad has to pay eight percent interest on what *he* borrows from the bank. If he borrows a hundred dollars, he has to pay back the hundred dollars *plus* eight dollars interest. So we have to pay *him* back fifty-four dollars. Most people are glad to pay for credit. Without credit, how would they buy big things like houses or college educations—or start businesses?"

"That's four dollars out of our profits," moaned Andy. "But we'd better pay the interest, or we'll never get into the oil lamp business."

What's he griping about? In frontier times the interest was up to three hundred percent.

16 ★ Alice Finds a Dollar is Worth Less Than a Dollar

"Six months ago you charged only one dollar for the same job," Alice shouted at Peter when he asked two dollars for repairing her bicycle. "What makes you so greedy?"

"Don't blame me," said Peter. "Blame INFLATION. Prices are zooming on everything—milkshakes, jeans, haircuts, my workshop rental, and spare parts for bikes. Wherever you look, consumers demand more than producers can supply—or *will* supply—at the old prices."

"And now that prices are so high," whooped Andy, who worked for Peter, "I need a raise."

"See?" grunted Peter. "With all my expenses up, I have to charge more to stay in business."

"A dollar just doesn't buy what it used to buy," lamented Alice.

A dollar is like a balloon—the more you inflate it, the weaker it gets.

17 ★ Andy Feels Picked On

After Susan and Andy sold their batch of oil lamps and wanted to buy more, Susan's father said the credit would cost them ten percent instead of eight percent. "Why? Why? Why?" Andy shouted.

"The government forced banks to raise the interest rate," said Susan. "That's one way of battling inflation. Higher interest discourages people from demanding too many loans for houses, cars, and other expensive items."

"It discourages me all right," groaned Andy.

"Things could be worse," said Susan. "The government might also increase taxes—or even freeze prices and wages."

"That would clobber me," sighed Andy. "People would have less money to buy oil lamps. We wouldn't even be allowed to raise the price to make up for fewer sales!"

"What if the government cuts its own spending to fight inflation?" asked Susan. "People would lose government jobs or help. So don't be such a martyr about our oil lamps!"

Andy and the government—it's like a chihuahua and a mean Great Dane.

18 ★ *Hamilton Learns the Hard Way*

What good money Hamilton made selling his water colors! But one day, Susan, a customer, announced, "I can't afford paintings anymore. My Dad got laid off at the TV plant and cut my allowance."

"Why did he lose his job?" asked Hamilton.

"Don't you know about the RECESSION?" gasped Susan. "Everything is so expensive that people can only afford to buy necessities, like food. Ordinary purchases, like TV sets, have suddenly become luxuries. So factories that make these things had to cut down production and lay off workers. Unemployment is going up like crazy."

Pretty soon Hamilton found out for himself what recession meant. His other customers also stopped buying paintings. He was out of work.

Recession is like someone sticking a pin into your balloon!

19 ★ Hamilton Blames the Government

"It's the government's fault," said Hamilton, explaining why he was out of work. "The government could stop the recession."

"Oh really!" scoffed Alice.

"Honest! It could lower taxes and interest rates. That would give people more money to spend, and demand for all sorts of things would go up. Jobs would increase. People could buy paintings again, and I'd be back in business."

"Maybe the government will *create* jobs," said Susan. "When lots of people are unemployed, the government sometimes pays them to work on public projects, like building roads or hospitals."

"*Any*thing that stops recession is okay by me!" grinned Hamilton.

Hamilton and the government—it's like a chihuahua and a friendly Great Dane.

20 ★ Turn the Economy Upside Down!

"The cures for recession and inflation sound so complicated that I have to make a chart," said Hamilton, bending over a big drawing pad. "During the recession people bought only essentials."

"During inflation," said Alice, helping him, "prices soared."

"When either inflation or recession gets so bad that people suffer, the government tries to help by reversing what is going on," said Hamilton. After a pause he held up the finished chart for Alice to see.

What Government Tries to Do

To Cure Inflation the government tries to decrease demand by:	*To Cure Recession* the government tries to increase demand by:
• increasing taxes	• lowering taxes
• increasing interest rates	• lowering interest rates
• cutting government spending	• increasing government spending
• freezing wages	• letting wages float
• freezing prices	• letting prices float

21 ★ *An Economic Mystery*

Alice looked at Hamilton's chart. "But this doesn't show what government does when we have inflation and recession *at the same time*."

"Everyone thought that couldn't happen," sighed Tony. "But it did. And all the economic wise guys could do was give this new situation funny names like INFLUMP or STAGFLATION."

"Not even the President knew what to do," said Penny, "because anything you do to curb inflation seems to deepen recession. And anything you do to get rid of recession seems to heat inflation."

"If nobody can figure it out," wailed Hamilton, "how can I fix my chart?"

"Your chart is good enough," Tony consoled him. "For an unusual mix of conditions—like inflation and recession at the same time—you can probably juggle the cures. Economy is as full of mystery and changes as people are."

Throw out the chart! Try a crystal ball.

22 ★ *On the Move*

"What kinds of changes?" Hamilton cried despairingly.

"Technology changes economy," said Tony. "An invention can zip an unimportant company to wealth. Politics alters economy. Will a politician help cure inflation by voting for higher taxes during an election year?"

"Economy is people," said Penny. "Once you could hire women and children cheap. Now child labor is illegal and women demand equal pay."

"Economy is psychology too," Tony added. "People might hoard sugar because of a crazy rumor that sugar is going to be scarce. Then the *hoarding* makes it scarce! Economy is even weather. What if a drought ruins a wonderful corn crop?"

"Stop it! Stop it!" yelled Hamilton.

"So old economic rules can be smashed," Tony went on. "Although prices *usually* fall during recession, giant corporations might jump prices and big labor unions raise wages. And if their product is something people need, consumers have no choice but to pay more."

Smash old rules! Variety is the spice of economy.

23 ★ GNP

"If you say a person is rich," said Andy, "you count his money, his property, and maybe—if he's a big singer or writer—his talent. But how do you figure out how rich a country is?"

"Same way," replied Susan. "You count everything a nation produces in one year with its land, capital resources, and people—the total output of goods and services. That's called *Gross National Product*, GNP."

"You count all the peaches," chanted Alice, "and tractors and hats and band-aids."

"And television repairs," said Tony, "firemen's rescues, and waiters' services."

"Those are all VISIBLE," smiled Susan. "But you also have to count the INVISIBLE things—like credit, insurance, and patents."

"And the more a country produces," said Alice, "the higher its GNP is."

"And the higher a nation's GNP," said Tony, "the more clout it has in the world."

GNP	
United States	$1,155,200,000,000
USSR	$ 394,125,000,000
France	$ 217,810,000,000
Ghana	$ 2,572,000,000
Thailand	$ 7,684,000,000

(Data are for calendar year 1972 converted into US dollars)

24 ★ More Than One World?

"How many worlds do we have?" asked Andy.

"Dummy!" said Penny. "One earth, one world."

"Two worlds," objected Susan. "Economy has created capitalist and socialist worlds."

"Three worlds!" cried Peter. "The developing countries in Africa, Asia, South America, and the Middle East form the THIRD WORLD!"

"Four worlds," said Alice. "You can't lump together *all* developing countries any longer. Some Third World nations are earning lots of money from oil—so they'll soon have enough schools, hospitals, and highways. But there's a FOURTH WORLD—developing nations without money from oil—where people are starving."

Enough! Time for a countdown!

25 ★ One New World?

"Don't worry about poor nations," said Penny. "Rich countries send them money, food, and medicines all the time."

"Third and Fourth World nations say that's not enough," answered Alice. "They claim countries like ours have exploited them. Now they want a NEW ECONOMIC ORDER—a redistribution of all the wealth on the earth."

"How are they going to get it?" asked Penny. "With guns?"

"With people power," said Alice. "They have millions more people than we do. And with resource power. They have natural resources we need—oil, copper, tin, or bauxite. What if they put their human and natural resources together against our capital resources?"

"Blackmail us by not letting us buy natural resources we need?" shuddered Peter. "Start a worldwide people's revolution?"

"Economy shouldn't divide the world," said Penny. "Rich and poor, capitalist and socialist—countries should work together in the United Nations to make the earth one peaceful world for everyone."

Man, not dog, should be man's best friend.

26 ★ *Zero Growth*

"I loved Holland," Susan remarked when she got back from Europe. "Everything there was so neat and clean."

"And tiny and cramped like a dollhouse!" said Tony. "I'm for a BIG country like the United States, with space for bigger and better cities, highways, industries, and sports arenas."

"Until you run out of land and other resources," objected Peter. "We've already got crowded cities, water shortages, and wilderness disappearing under concrete."

"And why is bigger better?" asked Susan. "Bigger cars and factories mean more waste and pollution. It's not worth having everything ugly just to become richer."

"Why don't we have ZERO GROWTH?" suggested Alice.

"Alice is going nuts," scoffed Tony. "How can you stop growing?"

"Like in a spaceship," Alice explained. "Once passengers board a spaceship, they have to rely on their life-support system. If they can't make this support system grow, they can't pick up any more passengers. Isn't the earth like a huge spaceship in the universe? So unless we find new resources on the earth, we must stop growing bigger—zero growth."

Think small.

27 ★ *Freedom and Progress*

The United States has the most powerful economy in the world. Yet critics say capitalism can only build a rich, not a just, society. Along with liberty come risk and inequality: People can be comfortable one day and lose their jobs or investments the next day. Some people get much more wealth than others, sometimes only through luck or by birth.

Socialist countries claim to be more just—spreading riches more evenly so there is less class contrast in everything from clothing to vacation resorts. Usually citizens can rely on job security and sufficient old age care. Yet critics say that socialist governments achieve equality and security by making all the decisions and clamping down on personal freedom and comfort.

In the past, free citizens—free to elect their governments, free to choose their own livelihoods and lifestyles—have prospered most. And when new priorities arise, people who are free to speak and to protest can adapt faster than can people who must wait for a government verdict. So in the future, even though capitalists may turn more often to the government for help, they stand a good chance of improving the economic *quality* of life.

Understanding economy can pilot you to a richer life.

Index

	DATE DUE		

330
Rie   Riedel, Manfred
A kid's guide to the
economy